ZEUS AT TWILIGHT

Poems by
Will Walker

BLUE LIGHT PRESS ◆ 1ST WORLD PUBLISHING

1ST WORLD
PUBLISHING

SAN FRANCISCO ◆ FAIRFIELD ◆ DELHI

ZEUS AT TWILIGHT

1ST WORLD LIBRARY
PO Box 2211
Fairfield, IA 52556
www.1stworldpublishing.com

BLUE LIGHT PRESS
www.bluelightpress.com
bluelightpress@aol.com

BOOK & COVER DESIGN
Melanie Gendron
melaniegendron999@gmail.com

AUTHOR PHOTO
Jane Underwood

FIRST EDITION

Library of Congress Cataloging-in-Publication Data

ISBN: 978-1-4218-3650-8

ACKNOWLEDGMENTS

Some of these poems have appeared previously in these versions or slightly different versions in *Alabama Literary Review, Burningword, Chagrin River Review, Crack the Spine, Diverse Arts Project, Forge, Haight Ashbury Literary Journal, Hartskill Review, Passager, Pennsylvania English, Rougarou, Schuylkill Valley Journal of the Arts, Slow Trains,* and *Studio One.*

TABLE OF CONTENTS

I.

II.

III.

IV.

V.

VI.

For Valerie, always

*No more dead than yesterday, no more
alive either. Just about the same.*

— Philip Levine

*Yesterday I realized I've gone through most of my life
half-asleep. And now I'm resolved to go through
the rest of my life half-awake.*

— William Burdwood

I.

AT THE ROCK AND ROLL HALL OF FAME

We were young, and we were improvin'
— John Mellencamp

The clothes on the wall speak a simple,
shocking truth: I'm much too big

to be a rock star. These duds of Jimi
and Janis and Grace, even what we thought

was the mammoth Mama Cass, so huge
she might have needed a crane to keep her

enormous jiggling bulk from falling
through the feeble timbers of the strongest stage —

they're all munchkin drag, shrunken rags of tie dye
and stuff constructed from your grandmother's

Victorian parlor curtains. Too tiny to contain
my life-size form. My early history is history,

remote as the midgets who fought the Revolution
or the mutton-chopped subjects of the Civil War,

frozen in Brady's formal photos or splayed
in the trenches, blood turned to a lifeless syrup

fit only for the worm farm. Let's dwell instead
on the dreams my music heroes held,

hopes so huge they towered towards the cumulus,
stoked meditations on ourselves and our Gods

at the center of the molten crowded universe,
seething and alive, uncontainable, on fire.

WHAT THE DEAD DO BEST

The dead release us when they die.
We do not know it for a while,
we think we hear their voices,
we think they linger in the shadows of cats.

We think we become them, the way
they sneezed, the way they pruned
their roses. And yes they may be with us,
but now so far in love with the world

they watch us raise our glasses to them
and think *Ah, a perfect earlobe,*
Oh, the rippling sound of laughter,
the fine perfection of fingerprints!

Then they do what the dead do best: watch a bud
grow to a leaf that lasts a green season,
then free itself in a brief, lit symphony
and recreate itself as loam.

They love to watch a wave
stretch a thousand miles, pulse
over a whale, lift plankton near Greenland,
then build and break across
the patient sand. They breathe

in centuries. They follow dawn's
birdsong around the globe
for decades. When we feel the need, they drift
into our sleep and light our dreams.
At dawn they leave us, ships disappearing
at the horizon of a darkened sea.

THE DAMAGE DONE

The sun is a big book
filled with brave tales.
It broadcasts hope over the land.
The trees stand basking in the light;
they form a choir of immense subtlety,
a chorus choreographed by the wind,
planting strength in the earth, stirring the stones
to talk in tongues.

But the storm has felled scores
of splintered giants splayed on soggy fields,
forests left leaning, losing their grip.
They still love tales that span decades,
sagas of the seas rising up
to overthrow the wicked, oceans of grass
hallowing the scenes of massacres.
However little life is left, they stand
with their emperor, the sun,
and the budding flames of spring.

DAYDREAM

Hell yes, put me on a beach with no words
and a few crabs, gin-clear waters,
waves conducting the only colloquy,
clouds raising the only questions.

Why are we here? asks one dark cumulus,
and another, light-struck, perhaps thinking itself
part of the mind of God,
replies: *Because we are,
we are.* The ocean reflects it all
on its own shimmering skin, and it's clear:

To be is holy, to nap, divine. To wake
like Yahweh after His first Sabbath
and touch your lips to a cool umbrella cocktail —
or at the dawn of another untroubled day,
a nice hot cuppa Joe — is to enter a new universe
that needs only the sound of *Ahhh* to be complete.

Time does not pass, because it does not yet exist.
Memory is a dream as distant as dolphins
swimming circles around the great cetaceans
on the other side of the island, where krill drifts
in shoals ten miles wide and humpbacks
serenade the deep, sunless depths.

WHAT TRIBE?

From Lascaux, we see portraits of the animals:
lithe, nimble, spirited. Less often, the outlines
of the hands of the makers: ghosts of hands, fingers

spread, outlined in stippled pigment. Little sermons,
perhaps: anonymous makers, long since gone,
reaching out into the cave's still,

dark future. And we reach back, press
into their prints — smaller palms, shorter fingers,
but still the same evanescent flame of flesh,

asking the same questions: Who are you? What tribe?
What can you tell us? And why do we feel
the filigree of fingerprints pulsing

in the cold cave wall? If you listen
you can hear them breathe while they work,
spattering their fingers to make a mark and then carefully

lifting the blood-warm stencil, flexing cold fingers,
grasping a sputtering torch to find their way, step
by step, back to daylight and restless sky.

ETYMOLOGY

In his magnum opus, Geography, *the Classical Greek
natural historian Strabo wrote of the Meander (a river in
southwest Asia Minor) that "its course is so exceedingly
winding that everything winding is called meandering."*

Some days (today; tomorrow;
    a pocketful of others)
        you wish to be like that river.

Imagine standing
    on its banks. The river
that gives us

the word for bend in the road,
        twist in the river, winding
    from tongue to tongue,

generations of — who knows? —
    Turks to Greeks to Romans
to the scary Dark Ages. It flows through

plagues and starving
    and the Holy Roman Empire,
        within hailing distance

    of the Defenestration of Prague,
then back to Paris
    and a handful of King Louis,

then somehow crosses the Channel
          and the Atlantic — stowed
like a little bacillus in the scuppers

     of the *Mayflower*, shaking hands perhaps
with Squanto himself, making its
       way west across the mighty Miss'ippi. Bubbling

       in my little soup of brain, feline, twisting
rivulet percolating through the thousand
          generations of a foggy day.

CHOOSING A FONT

You want it readable, is all — and hospitable,
but what about the shape? Big, little,
round, square? Nothing snooty
that suggests a need for owlish lenses; nothing that smacks
of Ezra Pound, dragging the whole of Western —
and Eastern — culture along by its short and curlies;
no whiff of Eliot, leaving your reader paused
over the page, longing for a lethal dose
of cyanide, to get it over with.

Something that might make a young girl
look up from her park bench to wonder
if she's sitting under a sugar maple; something
to make a middle-aged man somewhere
pick up his dusty glove and decide to play
some catch; maybe a font that a dog
will rip to shreds, just for fun; a font
that will echo the ancient Chinese:
What follows is only what can be said in words.

II.

OUTSIDE THE WINDOW

I hate the living. You, dear reader, excepted,
pending analysis of some common problem areas,
beginning with odor assessment;
what the TV medical experts loved to call halitosis;
regrettable sports attachments;
political fixations; odd fits of snorting laughter;

an affectation of familiarity and love for the obscure tribe
of pygmies, gorillas, or nicotine-drenched Frenchmen
or demoiselles with whom you spent your adventurous twenties,
fighting off dysentery, climbing Mt. Kilimanjaro, and learning
to say *All men are brothers* in fluent and lyrical Swahili.

Tonight, though, right outside the window, lurks a figure
of the usual unfortunate sort, a little maelstrom
of insanity induced by God knows what cocktail
of hormonal, chemical, and circumstantial misfortune,
perhaps a spokesman for some truly psychotic deity
or fallen angel, the Hornèd One or worse. He's not malevolent
by plan but in such pain he curses at the shadows,
as if to cow them, herd them away from his stinking
threadbare foul-mouthed self.

And we — so the experts tell us, unless they're true followers
of St. Francis — can do nothing except stay inside, silent,
unmoved, enjoying the end of an uneventful day, hoping
for him to get help somehow, but first to please move on.

DISHWASHING OLYMPICS

Last, Walker soaps the whisk caked
with cocoa powder, rinses it clean
with the sink hand sprayer, then sets it
squarely in the utensil caddy on the drain board
to the right of the sink and flicks off the kitchen faucet.

He's through in record time! What economy of motion!
What focus! His dismount was flawless! The crowd
is hushed; you can almost hear the water draining
from the carving tray stacked on the back edge
of the sink. Incredibly, his two dogs

lie silently on the kitchen rug, unaware
of witnessing dishwashing history in the making!
Kitchen Stadium may never again behold
such a feat, at least not in this category:
Stone-Cold Sober, Post-Prandial, Solo and Solitary!

Walker seems a bit winded but proud —
and who wouldn't be? He's worked hard for this moment,
training with various commercially-available, unenhanced
dish soaps and sponges for decades, breaking uncounted
bowls and dishes, even the occasional wine glass.

He's sliced open a finger or two along the way, and shelved
an astonishing total of 6,258 pounds of cutlery, utensils,
plates, pots, and pans. He's earned his medal,
and his impending nap in the Olympic Village.
By all means, rest on your laurels, Mr. Gold Medalist!

BATTING PRACTICE AT STANYAN PARK

Somewhere close by just over a hundred years ago
someone is taking batting practice at Stanyan Park,
an hour before game time. Is it Lefty O'Doul, swinging

from the heels, launching ball after ball toward our front steps,
into the living room, or maybe creaming a real screamer
that bounces all the way into the backyard and settles

in the little kingdom under our apple tree? Hard to tell,
we're perched somewhere in the cheap seats removed
more than a century from the peanuts and Cracker Jacks,

somewhere deep in the outfield. Perhaps we'll never know
if it's left or center or right. Maybe it doesn't matter
where they stuck home plate, or if the Seals

ever played down the block, or if the field was still
green and tended when our house was built
before subdivisions and the Influenza and The Great War.

It was before Mickey Mantle's grandfather ever heard
        of baseball,
before Babe Ruth or Tyrus Cobb, when it was still
just a game, and someone who maybe knew my grandfather

in his prime was sitting in the stands talking about
        the real '49ers
and watching the high lazy flies leap off that long-since
        broken bat
and head into a future only a few hundred feet away,

but always out of sight, even if he squinted to see it.

DON'T CALL IT SURGERY,
IT'S JUST A PROCEDURE

One thing I know: They won't start
        without me. Absent, I'll still be

the star, or perhaps only the stadium
        in which the star performs,

though if that's what I am
        I'll be a quiet venue, I hope,

one deliriously sedated, I pray,
        knocked out and sent to await

my arrival in the recovery room.
        There some kindly granny sort

with the beatific smile of one
        from the Other Side will tell me

firmly but pleasantly to breathe —
        come on, lady, who needs help

with that, but thanks for setting
        the bar so very, very low

for reentry to the busy,
        conscious, beeping world

of medical contraptions. And then
        I'll lie there like a plucked chicken

and breathe, proud of my
　　　accomplishment, in love

with my newly recovered body,
　　　not yet inclined to do anything

except smile the cockeyed smirk
　　　of the still half-buzzed

while thanking my aged nurse
　　　with my drug-soaked lips and tongue

and newly liberated vocal cords.
　　　Thank you, granny, you are my

Mother Teresa, but without
　　　the distracting doctrinal issues

and the troubling Bride of Christ
　　　superstructure, just another

local angel of mercy, a sort of
　　　anatomical hatcheck lady,

giving me back my flummoxed
　　　arms and legs, my flesh, all

the unassuming baggage of my body.

MEDITATION ON HOUSEHOLD APPLIANCES

On my block this very afternoon is a handful of solitary souls
bonding with their refrigerators, thanking them
for keeping cool in the face of challenging circumstances.
They're adding a hearty *Thanks, old buddy* for not talking back
or getting heat rash or suffering from a loose crown.

Somebody's spouse somewhere nearby may be suffering,
but the fridge is just fine, a paragon of energy reduction,
efficient and even-tempered, unlike some people,
not to mention any names. And some days

that's what we all love about our household appliances,
that they don't talk back, simply making their own choices
as long as they are able. Then they fail, cheerfully,
without guile, souring the milk but never blaming you
for not drinking it, never making matters worse
by complaining about lapsed service agreements
or dust bunnies or the way you failed
to steady them when you had the chance.

WHAT ONE DAY TELLS THE NEXT

Before sleep I tidy up, wash dishes, invite
tomorrow's breakfast in, set up a little shrine
to cocoa and coffee and oatmeal. Upstairs,
sleep awaits, where dreams spirit me through
the mansion of my many years, ransack
hidden closets, resurrect so many dead — surprising
how lively, and so well — and mix scenes so vivid
you'd never guess they're from school yards
where I haven't skinned a knee in fifty years.

I am hapless there, unsurprised by talking dogs,
weightless and then unable to stay aloft, telepathic
yet tongue-tied — and, worst of all, without memory,
waking with no recall, only able to walk downstairs.
There I see the signs I set up for myself the night before.
The pots and dry dishes say nothing has changed,
my appliances still heat and cool and toast
and peel, just as they did before I sailed away
on my epic pilgrimage of sleep.

ODE TO SATURDAY

Day of infinite possibility!
You don your rose-colored glasses.
Why not? Is it now a crime
to want to warm up
the sunshine, to build
a toasty glow of firelight
around the morning,
to cozy up to your dozing
Jack Russell, at rest,
solid as a loaf of bread?

Then you shed your office clothes,
your titles and obligations.
Think of the burden
of being king or president
or minister, time always breathing
down your neck, power
and position and the welfare
of your people dogging
your every step!

You head toward hours of delicious
slack, empty, unscheduled minutes
to block out like a painter
with a bright palette and something
important to say about a leaf,
a little oblate, something pointed,
spear-like, a curved edge
like a blade, a thing fallen
from a whole colony like itself.

Now it's unique, detached, its own
brief soliloquy, ancient as the Greeks,
an arrowhead from an Indian mound,
a mathematical formula made vegetal,
green turning to red turning
to dust with such silent grace. It's enough
to make you want to stop
all the clocks, and it's still
only Saturday, not yet even noon.

ODE TO SHEETS

Close the round book of the world
and open the volume
marked sleep.
Fold back the sheets
and lie down in an envelope
of night, a little folded package, the cocoon
that encases the butterfly
of dreams. Neruda has written
an ode to beds, but he forgot
the sheets, and so he tosses
and turns in the prickly
tangle of blankets
and mattress pads like a convict.

Ah, sheets! Imagine the inventor
of sheets, one smart woman,
adorning her bed and smiling
to her lover or mate,
I have sheets. Come, lie down
on these, luxuriate, feel them
like a second skin, a silk shirt
of sleep, a Persian carpet of dreams.

We sigh and want to drink mimosas
and wake to the smell of bacon
and the bright, clean hymn
of morning sun sparking
on dew. Sheets! So much
to forget about thread count
and fabric, the harvest of cotton,
the warp and weft of commerce!
So much to recall about the dark
consummation of night.

DAILY FARE

I chose oatmeal this morning as I always do;
it's a marriage, a ritual, something I substitute
for prayer, good hygiene, civic pride
and a responsible, disciplined life.

I don't smother my oatmeal
with these extensive extras, or top it
with fruit and nuts and vitamins and righteousness.
Oatmeal is a food of my ancestors, some of them,
Scots buried in churchyards I can only imagine,
speaking with a burr I can hardly decipher,

but, god, you know they loved their oatmeal.
You'd have to, to make haggis out of it,
the world's most maligned food, except for
Rocky Mountain oysters and no doubt
some obscure delicacy from New Guinea,
cow's bladder marinated in raven guano
and topped with especially prickly thistle.

No, I eat my oatmeal straight, no chaser,
no expectations, just the satisfaction of saying Hi
to the ancestors and nothing more.
It's a perfect food to eat alone, in silence,
while waiting for the brain to clock in,
suit up, pick up that scary, searing blowtorch

and begin shaping the cold, hard steel
of morning into something with holes in it,
maybe a moon, some stars, a stealthy fox,
and an expanse of something uncharted,
the windswept, quivering heath.

.

III.

SOME SIMPLE PLAN

A green day: You want that.
      Not the green of impending storm,
           clouds layering the neighborhood

with a light that says *Close your windows*
      and await the deluge. The green of redwoods
           and eucalyptus. The green of long silence

and footpaths cushioned with peaceful detritus.
      The green of deep, untroubled breaths exhaled
           in a forest that has done nothing but praise the earth

for centuries, and harbor mists that burn off
      in the tranquil light of morning. Some simple plan:
           Reach the ridge by lunch and sit with a sandwich

and some water. Survey that city to the south,
      so far away it looks intentional, every block a tight essay
           in civic planning. The panorama tells a soothing story

of commerce and inquiry held at bay
      by the silent footpaths of deer and the precarious
           teetering of hawks and buzzards catching the updrafts,

searching the hillsides for signs. Then perhaps
      some talk, a new take on the folks back home,
           a new embrace of all your life, even the bad.

And then an unhurried descent by a brook
      only a fool would say was babbling when it's clear
           the water clings to each rock like a prayer.

SOME THINGS I LIKE ABOUT LEAVES

for Jane Underwood

They have no Twitter accounts.
Are unconcerned about all the social networking sites.
Will never write an article entitled *Ten Ways to Preserve
      Your Cellular Beauty.*
Have never read *War and Peace.*
They are unaware of Ashton Kutcher and Madonna.
Have never heard of Adolf Hitler.
Some of them do have a soft spot for Walt Whitman,
      however.
They fall down without a sigh, and lie littering the earth
      without once struggling to get up.
Leaves do not listen to the radio in their Humvees or low-
      riders with the bass so loud it shreds the diaphragms
      of pedestrians halfway down the block.
They are the earth's dream of flight,
the wind's incarnation of dance;
the voices of the souls of the dead.
Leaves are the future of humus and the saviors of our topsoil.
Large or small, they never go to their graves wishing they had
      worn purple, or kissed Nan Gardiner or Jimmy O'Reilly
      in seventh grade at recess.
They never, ever drink too much at office parties.
All spend their days appreciating the light.
They are kindred spirits of the stars.
They whisper in a thousand different tongues.

IN WHICH I THROW A SNIT, BUT
THE WORLD FAILS TO NOTICE

Currently I'm mad at the world, but the world does not ap-
pear
to be mad at me. Though I am not returning calls,
friends phone to ask after me.
                                The world is a big room,
an enormous spool of day unwinding into night,
filled with several arks of creatures that wish me
no harm.
                 Nematodes by the millions.
                                    Even a few
of the strains of bacillus that might kill me
if they could, don't even know my address.

The monks in Katmandu think I have led
virtuous lives aplenty to be so blessed.

A million or more Haitians would kill to sit
in front of my TV and brood about the tax man
who's out to get me,
                         the loan officer
oppressing me with reams of paperwork,
and the city that wants its taxes on time.

Young men in the Czech Republic
or whatever state it has become
                              would perk up
to hear I live in fabled San Francisco, city
of thousands of happy freaks.

I am so outvoted by the Ethiopians,
who don't know that I exist,

                                but would devour
the contents of my refrigerator with celebration,

dancing perhaps, singing a song of praise
to God the Bountiful, purveyor of infinite mercy.

The dark cloud above my head, one can only think,
might pass in an instant if I could but spend lunchtime
with my distant cousins
                                in the Gobi Desert,

drinking yak butter tea and warming myself
at their tiny fire of dried horse dung.

But I remain unmoved by the news of Kenyans
                happy with nothing other than a colorful shirt
and a catchy tribal ditty.
                                The Kenyans, it must be said,
carry on much too merrily, swatting flies,
blinking dust from their eyes,

loving the same earth, tracking the same sun.
                Cranky as I am, I could never hate them for this.
                They are so busy surviving, they make me wonder
if I even exist.
                Or this ephemeral snit.

LONG AGO, FAR AWAY

You rent a house in the woods
and spend the winter wondering why.

Just down the hill, a gravel pit
has eaten a crater in the land.

A few saplings hang on at the edges,
roots still sucking air, though doomed.

Down past the pit, by the silent
and busy river, a stand of pines grows

on a little flat ledge. So many, they are old
before their time, each one pressed so close

to its neighbor they creak like the bird-thin
legs of octogenarians. There is barely

any life left here, except when the snow
blankets everything in prayer, the silence

of meditation, the rhythmic breathing
of the dead. In snow the world shrinks

down; you see a spider, trapped
in a gleaming expanse of crystal flakes,

making her painful way among rainbows
everywhere, and you can only try

to bless each delicate step, each moment
a ballet beckoning its own end.

A MARRIAGE

Gallantly, you sleep on the wet spot. You dream
and awake to the miraculous and strange: a marriage,

"relationship," what that weird kid in the quirky movie
calls "spanning time." Somehow you persist,

"you" now a plural being, sometimes at peace.
Sometimes now it seems sleeping

is what you do best; sometimes it's a miracle to make it
through the night. And there is mystery. It's everywhere.

Days pass, and years. You are not the people you once were,
though you remember them, often in a kindly way,

the way an old lover comes to mind and you speak to her
tenderly, wishing you had done that forty years ago, before

you drifted off into your own stories and changed
even your names. And the changed

selves you've married again and again are so surprised
by the new people they have become.

THE THING WE ARE BEFORE
WE KNOW OUR NAME

You see it in babies sometimes, their jewel-like hands,
too tiny to be the tools of cartilage and bone
and new muscle, too soft and new to be the willing,
careful servants of thought: The hands reach out, following
the blurry direction of new eyes, unfocused yet wide,
seeing something so luminous it's impossible to describe.

And of course there are no words, there is barely cooing
from the fresh, surprising vocal cords, and drooling,
and the eyes leading the hands to rise in a little
surprising hosanna, reaching for something we may
never fully grasp, the whole perplexing blur of light,
the simple Isness of the world. It's the thing we are

before we know our name, the brilliance of something
like a soul slowly downloading into a mind, a brain,
fingers and toes. The fingers fan out and flex in a gesture
I can sketch in some language but would prefer
to inhabit once again, wordless, from within.

SHORT STORY

Start with a question — say, *Where does this pencil
come from?* Then imagine for a moment
the little symphony of stories attached —

the graphite, sweet cedar, glue that sticks
the wooden halves together,
factory that makes a flood of pencils even now,

foreman who comes home with the smell of cedar
in his hair, trucker who carts in the little steel jackets
that hold the erasers, the distant source of rubber

for the tips themselves. Soon
you have a world, several continents tingling
with the intricate tale, even before

you think about the woman in Peoria
using a pencil just like yours — a Mirado
Black Warrior, HB2, arrived

from only God knows where, or when —
who writes a cryptic note to her husband Jake —
Gone for smokes, back soon —

and walks out the front door into the evening
of a balmy summer afternoon.

BROKEN

You start a sentence. It stops. You stand
at the edge of an immense canyon.
You close your eyes. Her words wait
at the other edge. The silence is dark.
It trembles, then settles down.

Eyes open, you reach out for her hand.
You stay that way a long time, hands tight,
while you both stare through the car windshield,
as if finishing a long journey. There's nothing left
to say, and the silence says it. Your hand and hers, it seems,
will never come undone, and yet after a long time
they do, and she says, probably, Good-bye.

This is the last time you will see her climb
the front steps. This is the last time you will drop
her off. What happens next is what always happens.
Someone walks by, a stranger from another story,
a character you might have met once in a dream.
He is thinking thoughts you can only guess at,
and walking to a door you've never unlocked.
Tomorrow he'll wake to birdsong,
some breakfast, maybe a fresh start.

After he passes, the night is still.
You could sit here alone, but you won't.
Even now, you have someplace else to go.

IV.

THE GRASS IS ALWAYS GREENER...

Well, the grass is always greener in the other fellow's yard;
The little row you have to hoe . . . oh boy, that's hard!
— Big Brother Bob Emery

It's 1956 and I'm watching Big Brother sing his song,
the one about green glasses and the other fellow's yard

and I have no idea what he is talking about, but his ukulele
assures me he's enjoying himself and it doesn't make

any difference what it means, it's just something the old guy
does every day, right before he pours himself a nice tall glass
        of milk

and the mellow little organ starts playing the tune that
            turns out
to be "Hail to the Chief," although I don't know that yet.
        I just know

the way the little funky organ sounds punching out
            those chords —
dut, dut, da-dut, dut da-dut da-dut da-dah-dut — and I've
            never seen

a little skating rink organ before, and I have no pictures
            of skaters
whizzing by on the rink while Big Brother drinks his milk;
            in fact,

all I have is the memory of the photo of Ike, the balding
slightly confused-looking elder to whom Big Brother
            is drinking his milk.

And I have no interest in Ike, or in drinking milk,
          but this routine
seems to calm Big Brother, I think he actually drinks
          his big glass

of milk every day after saluting the president and cueing
the cheesy organ music, and I have no idea that while
          the camera

is focusing on the black-and-white photo of Ike perhaps
Big Brother is switching out his full glass of milk
          for an empty one.

I don't really care about any of it. I just know that Big Brother
is on TV, and I am watching on my own, and it's a weekday

and I'm in our TV room upstairs, with the porch and the
          blue canary
in the corner, and I don't recall if this is before I find

my father passed out drunk on his bed, stinking drunk,
when I stand in his doorway and look around in a panic,

wondering what I can do, knowing there's nothing to do,
knowing I'm all alone. That may not have happened yet,

and of course I don't know that the fifths hidden in the
          toilet tanks
everywhere are his, not the maid's, and I have no idea

where the rest of my family is, I'm alone with Big Brother
and his strange routine and his glass of milk and his moldy

old president and his strange theme song on the wheezing
little organ, and I have no interest in milk, because it's
          after lunch,

and still I watch Big Brother. Maybe he actually drinks
        his milk
before he puts the glass down and sighs with pleasure

in a restrained adult way and then cues up a cartoon,
probably Mickey doing something or maybe one of
        those strange

Warner Brothers cartoons with The Road Runner
        or Porky Pig.
Big Brother and I are all alone, I think, though maybe he has

an audience, a peanut gallery, rows and rows of little kids
        like me,
only these (if they exist) are squirming and maybe clapping

or drinking milk, who knows. I don't care about any of it.
It's already just a TV, something I grew up with, a black-
        and-white

set, not really black and white, more like some sort of
        off-green
darkling color and something lighter but not white, a shade

of gray, yes, the whole little box is a shade of gray really,
Big Brother and Ike and the milk, all shades of gray.
        But the ukulele

is sweet, though a little odd, and the organ is odd,
        and a little sweet,
and Big Brother Bob Emery's face is somehow angelic,

though I don't know about angels yet. He seems transported
to a place where there's just him and his milk and his organ

music and his picture of the president, and he and I
are there together, someplace far, far from home.

GOSSIP

We build houses
    to contain it,

but it slips out
in the night,

rounds the corner
to the package
    store,

loads up on
    smokes
and sweet vino,

staggers through
the zinnias,

rips down the
    trellis
of antique roses

after that,
then passes out

on the lawn
for all the
    neighbors to see.

Tsk
    tsk
        tsk.

Who would do
a thing like
that?

I APOLOGIZE TO MY SHIRT

Manboobs. Whoever thought? But in the light
of that shave at the ER, they cannot be denied.

Not yet a B-cup, but pendulous and feminine,
not a pec in sight. And so I apologize

to my manly flannel, deserving of a young man's muscle
and plenty of fresh air. Instead, well, I offer

one uncertain heart, prone to bouts of free expression
threatening the body's complex symphony, mixed

with a dose of flop sweat pressed from my life's
simplest acts — writing words on paper, coaxing

my cello to a simple song, speaking to bankers,
grocers, and the occasional medical professional.

You deserve a lumberjack or perhaps a Gary Snyder
distilling the essence of mountain stream

and peaceful campfire into a few little lines flavored
with a tincture of Zen. Fuck it, you get manboobs

and a ride on a big-city bus lurching through
the day, refuge (one hopes) to only a crazy or two,

a teen with a voice shrill enough to shatter glass,
and one odiferous gentleman with the creepy

malevolent eyes that make me oh so interested
in staring past my manboobs at my own scuffed shoes.

ALL SYSTEMS GO

Woke up this morning to the daily miracle:
my body, busy defending itself, not so much
as a memo necessary to me, its operator;
no text message saying Boss, all systems go.

When you get to seventy, my stepfather liked
to say, *if you wake without pain,*
you know you're dead. I've got perhaps
ten years to trot this little blood factory around

unhindered, peeking out at the neighbors,
finding new ways to touch the earth, celebrate
gravity, and practice the Zen of aging: letting go.
Wondering less about my third-grade years.

Savoring the memory of Ellen Burrows' snow–
white underwear. Dwelling in the dimly lit ardor
of my first kiss. Thanking the Doors
for the soundtrack to my first excursion
into the hinterlands of stonerhood.

And bowing to tomorrow, and tomorrow,
and tomorrow, as a parent might watch his child
drive away from home on his first solo run
across the next state line.

FOUR–EYES

As an ancient Greek I'd be blind,
not allowed a sword or shield,
certainly nothing like a spear.
The stars: a mystery.

Now I count as revelation the day I got my specs,
heavy dark plastic too nerdy for a third grader,
and stepped outside in the afternoon sun.
I looked into the highest bare maple next door
by the Adams' house and was astonished
by the branches, each twig fat with buds.

There should have been music, a symphony,
Beethoven's Fifth blaring — but no, only silence
broken by the cry of a jay in the neighboring elm.
I picked him out so easily I almost fell over
onto our pebbled driveway, dotted
with gray pea gravel, each speck casting
its own shadow. My own shadow

was so choreographed I thought I might
be performing a ballet the sun had organized
to celebrate my liberation. And that night,
after pork chops, I stepped outside again
to catch my breath and view the stars.

Infinity, twinkling through unscratched lenses.
I pushed my glasses up on my nose
for the first of a million times and saw
my breath turn to fog in the night air.

BEFORE THE WORDS

Before the song had words he sang it
the way the unborn shifts in the womb,
he sang it in his bones, he sang it through
his fingers as they walked along the frets,
feeling their way from chord to chord.

He stepped through a dark room he didn't know,
kicked the furniture, wrestled with a bulky sofa.
He lay down, exasperated. He slept the sleep
of the dimly restless. He spread out like a tidy green lawn
at midnight, then curled up next to his snuffling dog.

He watched the sun rise over the lake and thought
about the dawn, so peaceful before the dust rises.
He breathed the silence, listened for a word
and got one, and then a little chorus, and then the song.

The music stayed in his fingers, though,
the music was a smooth muscle, the ticker,
like his heart, the music was his breath
before the words, the tide drawing back
before it floods, the dark moon waiting for light.

WE NEVER COULD DECIDE

for my cousin, Dean, dead at fifty

I'd rather be deaf than blind, he said, and I said
I'd rather be blind than deaf, or was it the other way

around, it's decades now, but then we hoisted
our little sail and cast off and knocked around the bay

in a brisk southeast wind that pushed up
a few whitecaps until Pop! just like that the mast broke

on our little cat boat. No harm done really,
the local day-sailing party boat threw us a line,

overlooking our earlier taunts, and towed us
into shore. Crestfallen but unharmed, no one lost

an eye or limb. But deaf or blind?
We never could decide.

CAUGHT IN THE ACT

That crick in your neck: You test it, even though
the one thing the chiropractors agree on is, *Don't
test it! Don't! Test it! Don't!* And so you turn your head
right every chance you get while thinking, *Now! Now! Now!*

This time I know it'll be gone! This time my mind
will cure my neck! This time the healing will have begun!
This time or maybe next! Of course
your interest is scientific and healthy, you are
the steward of your own neck, you want only the best
for all manner of tissue over which you exercise

alleged dominion. But really you are your own little tyrant
and torturer, trying to force your neck to *Heal, dammit,*
or else *Suffer, baby*, you ungrateful little piece
of malfunctioning neuronal tangle and stone-hard bone!

You test until the conversation with your neck grows so tired,
you stop trying and do the one thing that might help:
You stop the palaver and hear your neck
now and then say, *Patience, mister: still a virtue.*

V.

THE CLEARING

A full moon
the scent of lilac

trees aligned
                in pilgrimage
around a new-mown
                     meadow

The evergreen night

I wake here
                in a dream
wordless
                observant

as the lone deer
that step by step
deliberate
                and care-
ful   emerges
at the meadow's edge

to listen
                for the pilgrim
        silence
of the evergreens

and my heart
gone wild
                with moonlight

THE GOOD PART

I'd like a Sunday
like a Mary Oliver
poem, with a few

perfect words and
lots of white space,
and paper with

a high rag content
and maybe some
righteous soy-based ink.

It would be a leaf
in one of her spare
little collections, with

a fine old lithograph
from the public domain
on the cover,

one that recalled the idyllic
Transcendentalist woods
of Thoreau and Emerson

and John Muir.
I'd like to stare
at the few

perfect words
close up with
my glasses off

and appreciate the clean
edges of the fine
big print and feel

like I'm in church,
the good part, when
the church is empty

and there's only
silence and the sound
of my own breath.

LIFE IN THE SLOW LANDS

Instead of standing at a ford
as the cavalry of your thoughts goes
charging through, throwing up spray
and muddying the stream
as it passes with guidons flapping, you feel

your mind slowly step from stone
to stone, hear the trickle of the water
mingle with the song of a sparrow
rinsing the dust off its feathers somewhere

upstream of you. You listen
as the light ripples around the edge
of the sun-warm smooth brown rock
you're standing on when the sparrow
starts its song.

Meanwhile, the cavalry has disappeared
in a cloud of dust.
You marvel at how they muddied
up the stream — and now it's hard to imagine
why they bustled by in such a rush.

SOMETIME AFTER BREAKFAST

Some days what's best said is nothing. Do the dishes.
Let the water rushing from the kitchen tap
and spattering in your fifty-year-old white porcelain sink
be your soundtrack, tuneless music, an aqueous rat-a-tat
little snare drum of busy bubbling strict time running

on and on. It tells you all about its full life, born
aboard a turbulent cumulus, accrued in the Sierra Nevada
in a hard, white winter attended by the tough mugs
of massive boulders and the ministrations of a forest
of firs, whole monkish colonies bearing witness
to snowmelt and trickle, a white field dissolving

into sedge and grass and wild orchids, a sea
of Indian paintbrush, phalanxes of forget-me-nots.
Then the deep absorbent meditation of earth,
and the engineered fugue of dam and pipes and valves,
followed by the burst of daylight and this happy exit down
a copper pipe, headed on a journey to begin again.

WHITE

After my father's death
I spent a winter in New Hampshire
almost snowed under with grief

that blanketed the woods
for miles and pancaked the kids' clubhouse
at the place where I stayed.

I floundered in an ocean of snow,
pierced by the beauty of dead things,
golden spears of grass

arrayed in impossible perfection,
the woods a wonderland of death.
Chickadees darted,

too busy to notice. And by the river,
night coming on, sometimes I heard
the sound of a train

on the far bank, couplings clanking
in the cold, headed somewhere
across a border, far away.

CONDOLENCES

I'm sorry for your loss.
Not sorry the way I'd be
if I had caused your pain.
And really, I have nothing
to apologize for, unless
to be human is to be sorry,
as if to share a common fate
is to create it.

So I'm not sorry in any
ordinary sense. I can't think
to say it any other way
is all. And your loss:
In what sense is it yours?
You, after all, are still alive,
except for the core that feels
newly dead, if it feels at all,
unless you believe in the soul,

though belief is slim comfort
in the light of whatever room
is now filled with absence
surrounded by a silence
that used to live and breathe,
eat and drink and say
the strangest things.

Still, though the words
can never really mean a thing,
and though each loss
is a mystery that does not explain
itself, or the one that
preceded it or the one to follow —

despite all that I don't know
and can't explain to myself
or anyone else, I'm sending words
that say I see death has visited you,
and nothing will ever be the same.

11/22/63

Everybody remembers the pink suit, says Steven Tilley,
its caretaker in the National Archives, quoted
in the newspaper. Even I, a man with no sense of fashion,

know these words to be incomplete. Everyone,
myself included, remembers the pink
Chanel suit with the matching pillbox hat;
everyone remembers the Chanel ensemble.

Not many know she fiercely refused to change out of her
Chanel ensemble after the assassination, because,
as the story says, she wanted everyone to see

what they had done to Jack. What they had done
was spatter his brains across the back seat
of his Lincoln and soak her pink Chanel suit
with its matching pillbox hat in his blood.

Later Lady Bird said, *I saw in the President's car
a bundle of pink lying on the back seat,
just like a drift of blossoms.*

LEARNING HOW TO LEARN

She says It's funny but the times of sorrow
have taught me most, and I say I think we
can also learn from joy, but I think I really mean
I can learn from joy, and would prefer it,
and she can learn from sorrow if she wants.

What can you learn from joy she asks
with impeccable logic and I flounder
as at sea, man overboard, because we all
know it's sorrow that softens us, grief
that opens our hearts, loss that lets us comfort
each other, that lets us know what love is.

We can learn from joy, meaning I want
to learn from it, I take it as my credo
that there are equal lessons, a happy life
is not one of diminished learning, vapid
or shallow. We can learn to share it, I say.
We can learn to feel it without apology
or fear. We can learn to give thanks
for the way sunshine brushes our cheek,
the way someone says the word *hyacinth*.

VI.

1959: THE WAY I REMEMBER IT

One of the big boys connects
and sends a fastball soaring
over the brick wall that is
the edge of the world.

(Our eyes can barely keep up!)
It bounces off the street beyond,
through the afternoon,

then comes to rest
among the gravestones on the other side,
white as bone, startling the dead.

GRIEF

It's a starless night
by the black Atlantic.

I'm standing in the ocean
up to my chest, cold and alone.

Under the neon light from the parking lot,
the waves pucker like scars on the sea,
hissing indifferently.

I hesitate, jostled by the spring waves
while I cast for something in the dark
and find enough of it
to chill me to the bone.

• • •

At his death, my father owned eight cars

— A battleship-gray Franklin,
1930, that I rode in once
when he drove it home

— a salmon-pink Willys jeep
to drive in the dunes
of the Cape

— a 190 SL Mercedes, two-tone.
dark gray & white with —
was it so? — red leather upholstery,
that I drove to school
once or twice, a second-hand

purchase from a co-worker

— the Buick 88, Newport green

— the Lincoln

— the VW van

— the VW bug

— the Peugeot

• • •

This is how things change:
He's driving in the old Army Jeep on the dunes —
my father — and all is well.
We're bumping through the dwarf forest
by the tumbledown Coast Guard station
and our dog Judy stands on the back seat
snapping at twigs as we
brush by. In a flash
she catches one & is pulled out
and under the back wheel.

My father stays behind
to bury her.
I see him kneeling over her
in his role as physician:
solitary and still.

• • •

I like to imagine
what might have been: that Continental,

the 1963, as a classic
with the simple associations
of, say, the Fleetwood Cadillac
with the spaceship tail lights
that got planted in a row
by that sculptor in Texas —
or even the Edsel, dog of its day,
the car Marianne Moore was retained
to name; she came up with lists
as abundant as ticker tape:
the Silver Thunderbird,
the Utopian Turtletop,
the Mongoose Civique. But Ford
in its corporate wisdom
chose Edsel,
named for Edsel Ford, a nephew
of Henry, or Henry II.
I want that Continental
to be the car in which JFK
rode to his second inauguration.

• • •

When my uncle took me to lunch
to talk about my mother
remarrying his old friend
quicker than you could say
he's dead and gone
and I tried to tell him of my sense
of loss, betrayal, and abandonment,
he looked sheepish & nonplussed,
shrugged in a way that was
actually avuncular
and said *I've seen stranger things.*

• • •

When I was five
and my father drove me to school,
he always made a detour
off the main road
onto a little half-circle
of a turnout he called
the racetrack.
Shall we go on the racetrack?
It's coming up. Here
it is, the racetrack.

The world's smallest
racetrack, a half-circle turnout,
fully paved, with a neat curb
and grass. Not my racetrack,
or ours, but his.

• • •

What happened to
my father's Newport-green Lincoln
I drove to the Cape
for a farewell tour before
surrendering it to the dealer
as a trade-in for my mother's
new white whale of a car?
Why didn't I just drive it
slowly into the sea?
Or buy it back and cruise
around in that cushy
bank vault of a chassis?
How did I just let it go?

DROWNING BY DAY

Dawn seeps
into the room
like water into
    a leaky boat.

Soon my sleeping craft
will sink into
the tide of light.

I will drown again
in day
and float among
the wrecks
of my past voyages,

the bare ribs
of crafts freighted now
with sunshine,
ghostlike, silent,
here and there
a shapely amphora,
a golden goblet
pocked with barnacles.

Each night I resurrect,
a miracle, and
build another leaky boat
to sink into the dawn.

THE LUMP

Just routine, her doctors say,
as if not knowing the routine
in which each day becomes
an endless tea party with Mr. Death,
a surprise visitor, always a surprise,
even if his calling cards
have mounded in a snowdrift
that obliterates the shiny silver tray.
Will you stay long, Mr. Death,
we ask, always polite,
not wishing to offend.

Just routine, her doctors say.
Mr. Death is obliged to attend,
but they expect no laying on of hands.
Her doctors breathe a mist
of antiseptic speech
that cloaks the act in which
they slice her breast, remove a lump,
sew her up, and leave a bruise
as solid as a fist.

Just routine, says Mr. Death
at the end of a quiet week.
Thanks for the tea, he grins,
no rush to restock my favorite blend.

FOR A CHANGE

Breathe.

Choose a simple cadence,
the easy rise and fall of the tide

against the rocky battlement of shore,
the way the water swells and fills

each crevice, each barnacle,
surrounds each hand of seaweed waving

in an absentminded dance.
Feel the way the silence floats

out of the sea. The way the swell
draws back, bowing to the rock.

Sure of its return, it takes its leave
with grace. Let go of all the rest.

Breathe.

THE PROBLEM OF SWITZERLAND

A pretty place
so orderly,
it keeps the peace —
like a museum

in a European city
whose streets are stacked
with the naked,
bloody corpses
of its citizens.

The curators
are clean, well-fed,
efficient to a fault,
but it is the crowds
outside the museum
bent on slaughter

who, now and then,
deliver up a David
from the chisel
of a Michelangelo.

FLYING WITH MY STEPFATHER

The dream doesn't care that he is dead,
just as it doesn't care that, technically,

defying gravity and rising up by the shore
would startle even a New Yorker. But that's

what I do: levitate, with the simple mental trick
that comes easily in dreams. Manhattan

or whatever city this is by what might be
a lake, is less crowded by air, and he

has joined me as I hover. I always liked that
about you, I tell him, that you weren't limited

by the rational, and he smiles with the ease
of a seasoned traveler, a man possessed

of the assurance that he comes from the center
of the universe, Manhattan, and is always

dressed for any occasion. And we
hover that way in the buoyant light.

ZEUS AT TWILIGHT

I wear a hat indoors now sometimes, just to keep warm:
faded blue with a yellow lightning bolt. Used to be
I heated up a room just by walking in. Retired now, really.
Don't misunderstand me, but the Jews ruined everything:
Yahweh this, Yahweh that, his bloated Hisness took over
the God business. And don't get me started on that Son of God
shit and that Mohammed character. Snake oil, I tell you.

Oh, I still hurl lightning bolts with the best of them,
but nobody seems to notice. They all think they're scientists
now, talking meteorology and low pressure and relative humidity,
like the world is some chemistry experiment.
I'm an oxcart god in a digital world.

I miss the Trojan War, really, but some change is for the good.
No more of that Leda and the Swan nonsense,
morals have changed a lot, and my cronies would laugh me
out of Miami if I dressed up as a bird. Now that I'm not so
high and mighty, I get along better with my wife,
and I sleep better without the din of prayers and imprecations
of the millions in my ears.

Not like the old days — Alexander running amok
over two-thirds of the known world, battlefields
where thousands died with my name on their lips,
hoping for safe passage to the afterlife. But fashions change,
I've had my day. Still, if you need me, look for me tomorrow
downtown on the street corner, playing some bottleneck:
faded blue cap, lightning bolt, singing a halting version
of "Nobody Knows You When You're Down and Out."

I'm no good, of course — Apollo's the musician
in our pantheon — but now and then an old fart
in sandals, white socks and a beret throws me a rumpled dollar.
I make sure his day goes well — coffee's hot, sun hits
his shoulders just right, he gets the last paper at the corner store,
and maybe a bright idea about walking home
the long way, through the park.

ABOUT THE AUTHOR

Will Walker was born and raised in Boston, Massachusetts, and spent his summers on Cape Cod, in Provincetown.

He moved to San Francisco in 1973 after exhausting all other options and has lived there since.

He lives in the Haight with his wife, Valerie, and their dog.

His poetry has appeared in *Across Borders, Alabama Literary Review, Alimentum, Bark, Burningword, Chagrin River Review, The Chiron Review, Conch.es, Crack the Spine, Diverse Arts Project, Forge, Haight Ashbury Literary Journal, Hartskill Review, Lame Duck, Passager, Pennsylvania English, Red Hills Review, Rougarou, Schuylkill Valley Journal of the Arts, Slow Trains, Spillway Revue, Street Sheet, Street Spirit, Studio One,* and *WriterAdvice*.

As a general summary of his life, he currently embraces these words from Berndt Oksendal's *Stochastic Differential Equations: An Introduction with Applications*:

We have not succeeded in answering all our problems. The answers we have found only serve to raise a whole set of new questions. In some ways we feel we are as confused as ever, but we believe we are confused on a higher level, and about more important things.

www.ingramcontent.com/pod-product-compliance
Lightning Source LLC
Chambersburg PA
CBHW032027090426
42741CB00006B/752